MY FIRST SCIENCE BIOGRAPHY

Jane Goodall

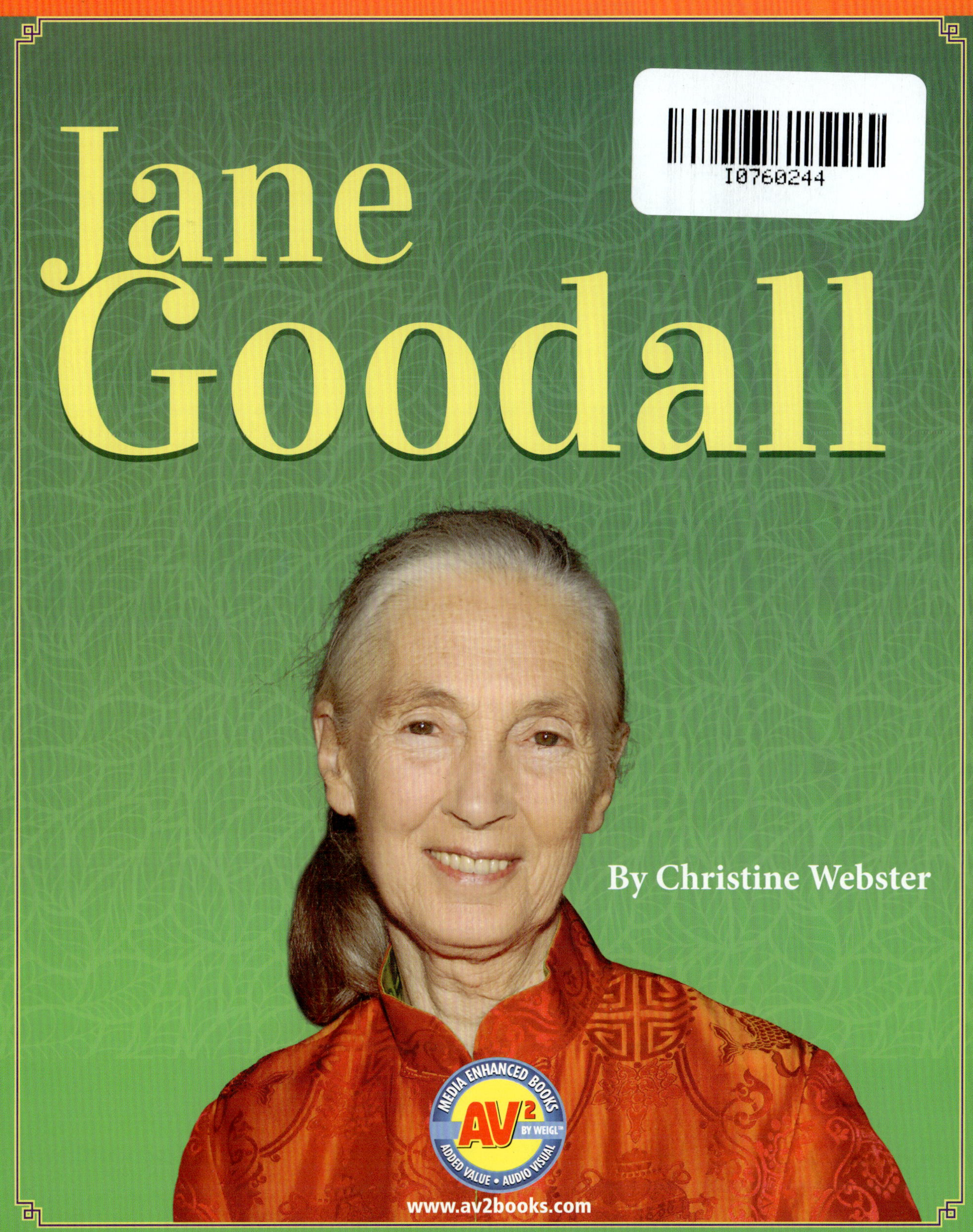

By Christine Webster

Go to www.av2books.com, and enter this book's unique code.

BOOK CODE

AVG82784

AV² by Weigl brings you media enhanced books that support active learning.

AV² provides enriched content that supplements and complements this book. Weigl's AV² books strive to create inspired learning and engage young minds in a total learning experience.

Your AV² Media Enhanced books come alive with...

Audio
Listen to sections of the book read aloud.

Key Words
Study vocabulary, and complete a matching word activity.

Video
Watch informative video clips.

Quizzes
Test your knowledge.

Embedded Weblinks
Gain additional information for research.

Slideshow
View images and captions, and prepare a presentation.

Try This!
Complete activities and hands-on experiments.

... and much, much more!

Published by AV² by Weigl
350 5th Avenue, 59th Floor
New York, NY 10118
Website: www.av2books.com

Library of Congress Cataloging-in-Publication Data
Names: Webster, Christine, author.
Title: Jane Goodall / Christine Webster.
Description: New York, NY : AV2 by Weigl, [2020] | Series: My first science biography | Audience: Age 8-9. | Audience: Grade 4 to 6. | Includes index.
Identifiers: LCCN 2019006536 (print) | LCCN 2019007836 (ebook) | ISBN 9781791111328 (Multi User Ebook) | ISBN 9781791111335 (Single User Ebook) | ISBN 9781791111304 (hardcover : alk. paper) | ISBN 9781791111311 (softcover : alk. paper)
Subjects: LCSH: Goodall, Jane, 1934---Juvenile literature. | Primatologists--England--Biography--Juvenile literature. | Women primatologists--England--Biography--Juvenile literature.
Classification: LCC QL31.G58 (ebook) | LCC QL31.G58 W43 2020 (print) | DDC 590.92 [B] --dc23
LC record available at https://lccn.loc.gov/2019006536

Printed in Guangzhou, China
1 2 3 4 5 6 7 8 9 0 23 22 21 20 19

062019
311018

Project Coordinator: Heather Kissock
Art Director: Terry Paulhus

Photo Credits
Every reasonable effort has been made to trace ownership and to obtain permission to reprint copyright material. The publishers would be pleased to have any errors or omissions brought to their attention so that they may be corrected in subsequent printings.

Weigl acknowledges the Jane Goodall Institute, Getty, Alamy, Newscom, Shutterstock, and Dreamstime as its primary image suppliers for this title.

Jane Goodall

Who Is Jane Goodall?

Jane Goodall is the world's leading **expert** on chimpanzees. She has spent years watching them and learning about how they live. Jane has been able to show the world that chimpanzees are smart, **social** animals.

Jane has also helped to save many chimpanzees. She has fought for laws that keep them safe. She works hard to make sure that chimpanzees do not become **extinct**.

"The least I can do is speak out for those who cannot speak for themselves."

Jane is an ethologist. This is a scientist who studies animal behavior.

Jane Goodall

Early Days

Jane was born on April 3, 1934, in London, England. As a child, she loved animals, nature, and exploring. When Jane was very young, her father gave her a toy chimpanzee. She named it Jubilee.

Growing up, Jane loved to read books about animals and Africa. Her favorite books were *Doctor Dolittle*, *The Jungle Book*, and *Tarzan*. Jane dreamed that, one day, she would study animals in Africa.

As a child, Jane once spent five hours in a hen house waiting to see how a hen lays an egg.

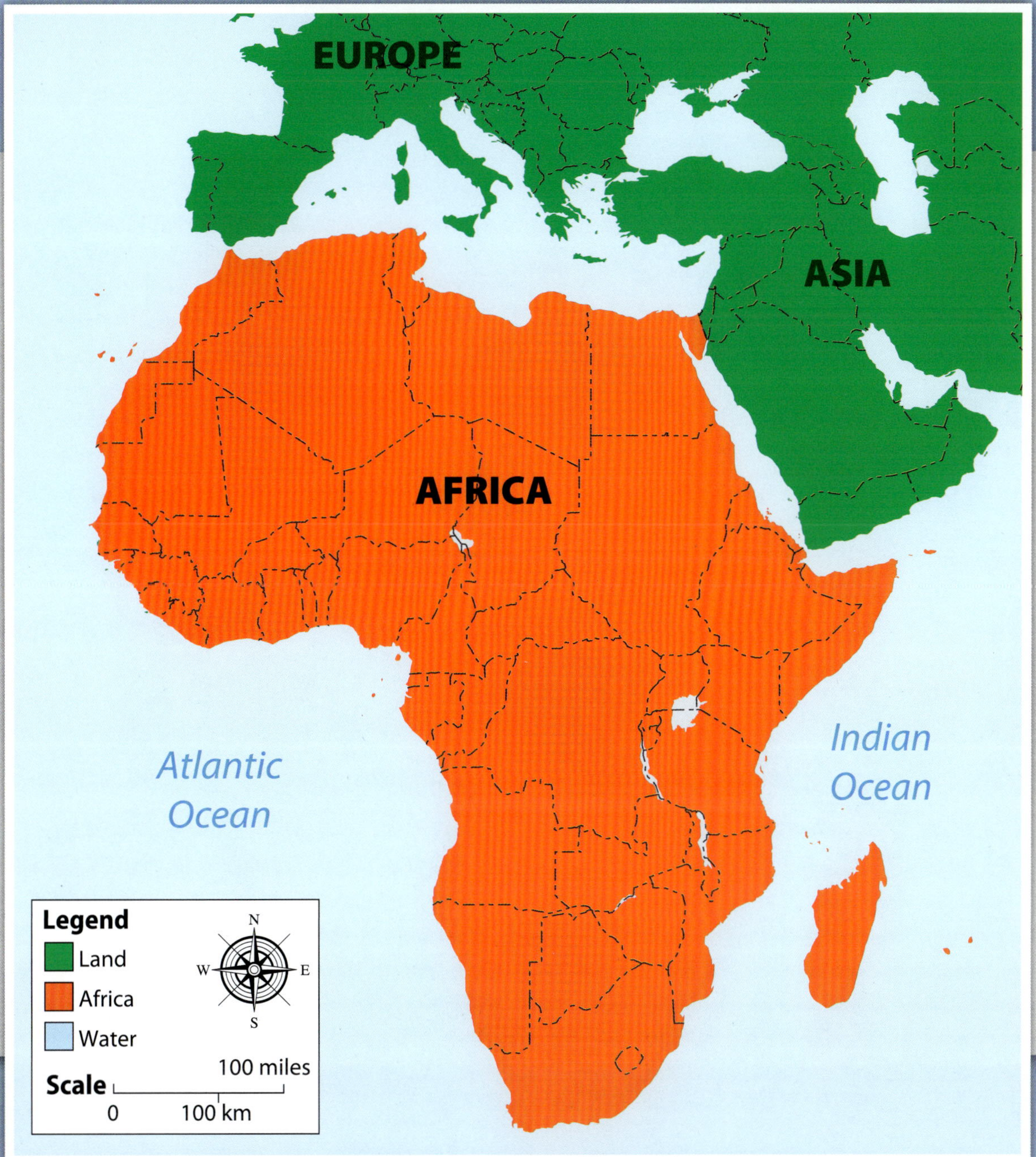

Where Is Africa?

Africa is one of the world's seven **continents**. It lies south of Europe and Asia, and north of Antarctica. Two oceans touch the coast of Africa. They are the Indian and Atlantic Oceans.

Jane met Louis after taking a job as a secretary in Nairobi, the capital city of Kenya. Louis worked at the city's natural history museum.

Starting Out

In 1956, a friend invited Jane to her family's farm in Kenya, Africa. She traveled there the following year. While in Kenya, Jane met Dr. Louis Leakey. Louis was an anthropologist. This is someone who studies humans and their ways of life.

Louis was studying chimpanzees as part of his work. He thought they could help him understand how early humans lived. Jane wanted to help Louis. She began working with him. In 1960, Louis sent Jane to Tanzania to study chimpanzees. Jane was only 26 years old.

Jane sailed by ship from England to Africa. The trip took **three weeks**.

Influences

Jane's mother was a key influence in Jane's life. She encouraged Jane's curiosity for animals and exploring. She even joined Jane in Tanzania. As Jane became older, she met other people who shared her interests and encouraged her study of chimpanzees.

Dian, Jane, and Biruté are sometimes called the Trimates. They were the first people to study great apes by living among them.

Dian Fossey

From 1967 until her death in 1985, Dian Fossey studied mountain gorillas in Rwanda, Africa.

Louis Leakey

Louis Leakey was the person who persuaded Jane, Dian, and Biruté to study **primates**.

Biruté Galdikas

Biruté Galdikas has studied orangutans in Indonesia since 1971. Her research continues to this day.

Practice Makes Perfect

Jane knew very little about chimpanzees at first. When she went to study them, some acted quite **hostile** to her. Others ran away screaming. Louis told Jane that she had to stay calm. He said the chimpanzees would be calm if she was calm.

Jane worked at staying calm. She watched the chimpanzees quietly and let them get used to her. The first chimpanzee to trust Jane was named David Greybeard. After this, many others trusted her as well.

Jane sat quietly in the same place every day. Over time, the chimpanzees became comfortable with her.

What Is a Scientist?

A scientist is someone who studies things. People who study animals are called zoologists. Scientists are very curious. They love solving problems. Scientists try to answer questions through **experiments**. They collect information using a six-step method.

Through her study of chimpanzees, Jane was able to prove that they have feelings.

Using a 6-Step Scientific Method

STEP 1

QUESTION

Scientists ask a question about what they want to learn. They read books and go online to research what other people know about the topic.

STEP 2

HYPOTHESIZE

The scientists then guess what the answer to their question might be. This guess is called a hypothesis.

STEP 3

EXPERIMENT

Scientists plan an experiment to see if their hypothesis is right. They gather the materials they need. Then, they set the materials up and do the experiment.

STEP 4

OBSERVE & RECORD

Scientists use their senses to observe what happens during their experiment. They watch. They smell. They listen, touch, and even taste. They then record what they find.

STEP 5

ANALYZE

Scientists think about what happened during their experiment. They decide if the experiment showed that the hypothesis was right or wrong.

STEP 6

SHARE RESULTS

Scientists let other people know about their experiment and what they found out. They may write a report or give a speech.

The Institute's youth program is called Roots and Shoots. It encourages young people to play an active role in making the world a better place for people, other animals, and the environment.

Overcoming Obstacles

Traveling to Kenya cost a lot of money. Jane had to raise the money to get there. She spent years working, waiting, and saving. When she got there, it was not easy living. She traveled for miles (kilometers) each day in the heat, following the chimpanzees. She lived in a tent in the jungle.

There were once more than 1 million chimpanzees in the world. Today, there are less than 300,000.

Over time, Jane saw that the chimpanzees were losing the land they lived on. People were moving into areas where chimpanzees lived. Soon, there would be nowhere for chimpanzees to live.

In 1977, Jane co-founded the Jane Goodall Institute. It has two main goals. The first is to protect chimpanzees. The second is to encourage people to do what they can to **conserve** the natural world that all living things share.

Achievements and Successes

In 2010, Jane was given a Bambi Award for her efforts in protecting the environment and the animals that live within it.

When Jane first began studying primates, there were few women doing this kind of work. Jane set an example for other women. Today, women are leaders in this field of science.

Jane's efforts have been recognized around the world. She has received many awards for her work. These include the Legion of **Honor** from France and Japan's Kyoto Prize.

Jane has received other honors as well. The **United Nations** named her a Messenger of Peace in 2002 and 2007. Many of the world's top schools have given her honorary degrees.

Jane received a lifetime achievement award at the 2018 Animal Hero Awards, in London, England. The award recognized her service to promoting animal care.

Workers at the sanctuary care for about 150 orphaned chimpanzees.

Jane visits zoos and other facilities to draw awareness to the issues facing chimpanzees.

Impact on Society

Jane has helped people understand that all living things are connected. She has taught people to respect nature. Jane has inspired people to do all they can to protect the natural world.

Jane still helps chimpanzees as well. In 1992, her institute built a **sanctuary** in Africa. The sanctuary gives chimpanzees a safe place to live. It also allows scientists to learn more about them.

Today, Jane spends about 300 days a year traveling the world, talking to people about the need to conserve the natural world.

Timeline

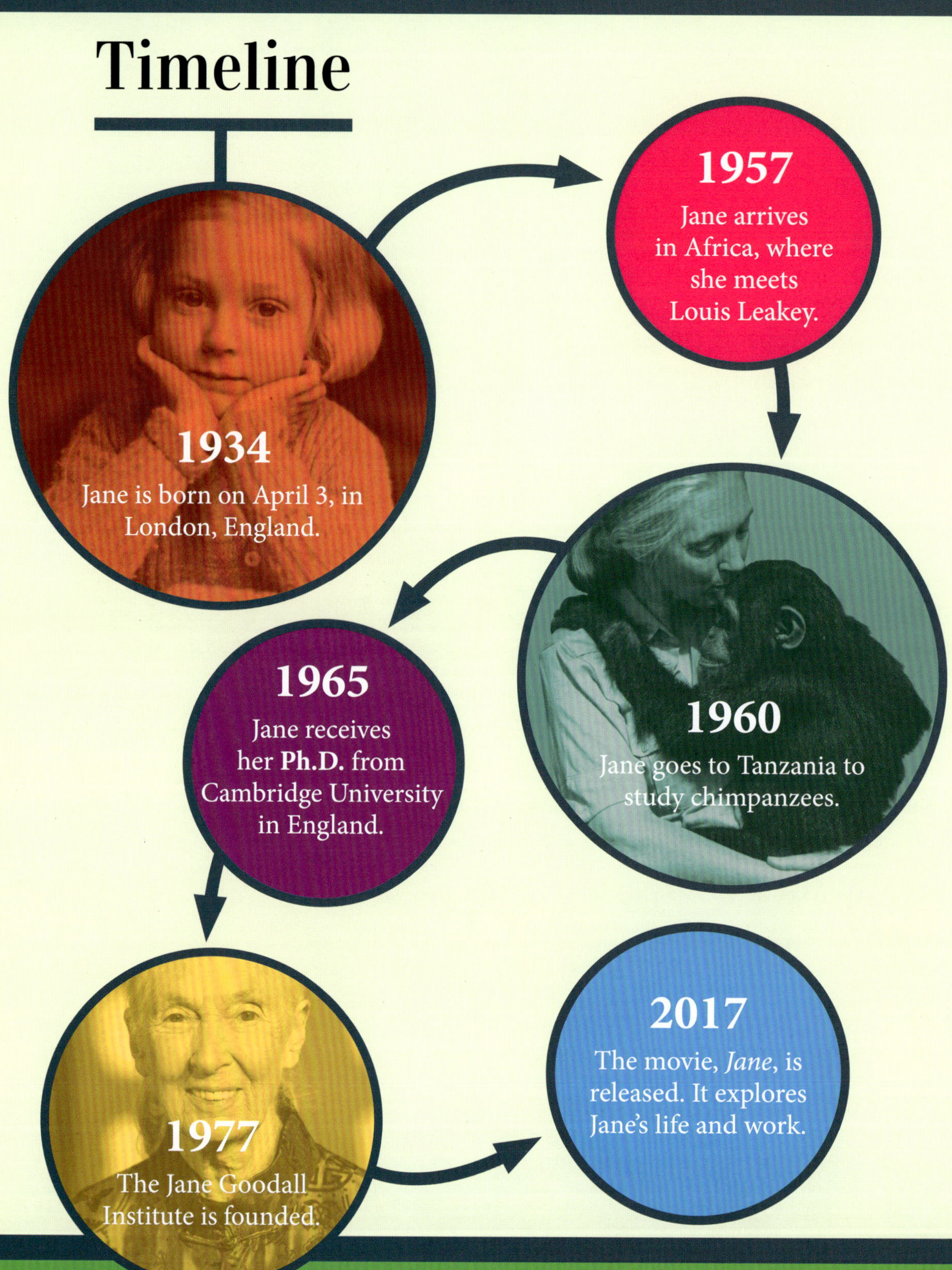
1934
Jane is born on April 3, in London, England.
1957
Jane arrives in Africa, where she meets Louis Leakey.
1960
Jane goes to Tanzania to study chimpanzees.
1965
Jane receives her **Ph.D.** from Cambridge University in England.
1977
The Jane Goodall Institute is founded.
2017
The movie, *Jane*, is released. It explores Jane's life and work.

Key Words

conserve: to keep and protect from harm

continents: the seven large land areas on Earth

experiments: tests that are done to prove a hypothesis

expert: a person who knows a great deal about a specific topic

extinct: no longer living on Earth

honor: a gesture of respect or appreciation

hostile: feeling or showing dislike

Ph.D.: an advanced university degree

primates: a group of animals that include humans, apes, and monkeys

sanctuary: a place where animals can live in safety

social: enjoys the company of others

United Nations: a group of countries that work together to solve problems

Index

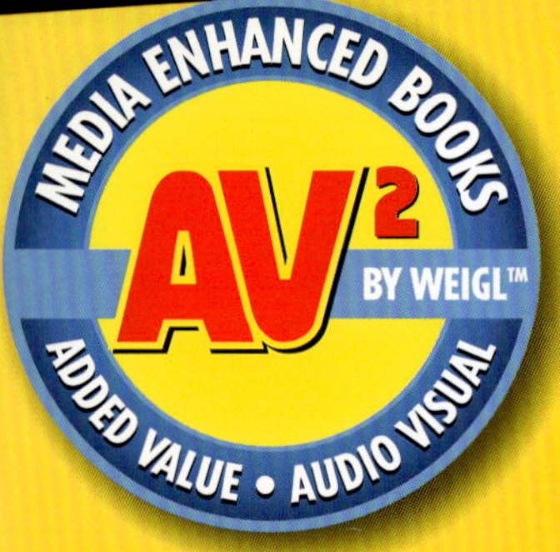

Log on to www.av2books.com

AV² by Weigl brings you media enhanced books that support active learning. Go to www.av2books.com, and enter the special code found on page 2 of this book. You will gain access to enriched and enhanced content that supplements and complements this book. Content includes video, audio, weblinks, quizzes, a slideshow, and activities.

AV² Online Navigation

Audio
Listen to sections of the book read aloud.

Book Pages
AV² pages directly correspond to pages in the book.

Video
Watch informative video clips.

Embedded Weblinks
Gain additional information for research.

Key Words
Study vocabulary, and complete a matching word activity.

Try This!
Complete activities and hands-on experiments.

Quizzes
Test your knowledge.

Slideshow
View images and captions, and prepare a presentation.

AV² was built to bridge the gap between print and digital. We encourage you to tell us what you like and what you want to see in the future.

Sign up to be an AV² Ambassador at www.av2books.com/ambassador.

Due to the dynamic nature of the internet, some of the URLs and activities provided as part of AV² by Weigl may have changed or ceased to exist. AV² by Weigl accepts no responsibility for any such changes. All media enhanced books are regularly monitored to update addresses and sites in a timely manner. Contact AV² by Weigl at 1-866-649-3445 or av2books@weigl.com with any questions, comments, or feedback.